STORMS

SEYMOUR SIMON

MORROW JUNIOR BOOKS
New York

PHOTO CREDITS
All photographs courtesy of the National Center
for Atmospheric Research—National Science Foundation,
except pages 6, 17, and 22, courtesy of the National Oceanic and
Atmospheric Administration, and page 28, courtesy of Richard Horodner.
Artwork on page 8 by Frank Schwarz.

Inquiries should be addressed to
William Morrow and Company, Inc.,
105 Madison Avenue,
New York, NY 10016.
Printed in Singapore.
1 2 3 4 5 6 7 8 9 10
Library of Congress Cataloging-in-Publication Data
Simon, Seymour.
Storms / by Seymour Simon.
p.   cm.
Summary: Describes the atmospheric conditions which create
thunderstorms, hailstorms, lightning, tornadoes, and hurricanes and
how violent weather affects the environment and people.
ISBN 0-688-07413-8.   ISBN 0-688-07414-6 (lib. bdg.)
1. Storms—Juvenile literature.   [1. Storms.]   I. Title.
QC941.3.S55 1989   551.5′5—dc19   88-22045   CIP   AC

To Joyce

We live at the bottom of a blanket of air called the atmosphere. The atmosphere is always moving, sometimes slowly, other times quickly and violently. These changes in the atmosphere are called the weather. We call the violent changes, storms.

Thunderstorms are the most powerful electrical storms in the atmosphere. In twenty minutes, a single thunderstorm can drop 125 million gallons of water and give off more electrical energy than is used in a large city during an entire week.

Each year, there are about 16 million thunderstorms around the world. Every minute, thousands of newly formed thunderstorms sweep across the earth's surface and lightning bolts flash 100 times a second.

Thunderstorms form when moist air near the earth's surface is heated by the sun. Like a bubble in water, the warm air rises until it reaches a layer of cool, dry air, where the moisture in the air condenses into tiny water droplets that form puffy cumulus clouds. The heat energy released by the condensing water causes a sixty-mile-an-hour updraft that draws more moist air from below. In minutes, the cloud may grow several miles wide and 40,000 or more feet high. Strong winds shred and flatten the cloud top into the familiar anvil shape of a "thunderhead" or cumulonimbus cloud.

The water droplets that make up the thunderhead grow by colliding and combining with each other. When the droplets become large enough, rain or hail begins to fall in a heavy thunderstorm.

The final stage of a thunderstorm is the most violent. The intense rain or hail causes strong downdrafts of wind. The updraft-downdraft combination is called a single storm "cell."

Some thunderstorms are visible as lone giants. But most thunderstorms are made of several cells in a row called a squall line. Each cell lasts for fifteen or twenty minutes, and then new cells replace old ones. Squall lines can last for hours.

A storm cell begins to die when gusts of cold wind blow the rain down and outward from the base of the cloud. The downdraft cuts off the updraft winds from the heat of the ground. Soon the rain slows and stops, and the thunderstorm spreads out and dies.

Thunderstorms are part of the earth's air-conditioning system. They pump heat from the surface high into the atmosphere, where it is released into space. Without this heat exchange, temperatures at ground level would be as much as twenty degrees warmer than they are now. Thunderstorms also cleanse the air and carry life-giving water from seas and lakes to dry lands.

Hailstones are chunks of ice that fall during some thunderstorms. Hail ranges from pea-sized pellets to stones the size of baseballs or even of grapefruits.

Hailstones begin to form when tiny particles of dust and ice collide with cold water droplets that freeze to them. The powerful winds of a thunderstorm toss these ice pellets up and down, and they grow larger as they come in contact with more water droplets. When the chunks of ice grow too heavy for the winds to carry them aloft, they plunge to earth as hailstones. This cross section of a large chunk of hail shows the rings of ice that make up the stone. More than twenty layers have been counted in some large hailstones.

Hailstorms sometimes cause great damage. Grasses and small plants are beaten into the ground by the speed and impact of the stones. Crops are broken and destroyed. Hailstones can knock down and even kill small animals such as chickens, rabbits, and squirrels, and they have injured animals as large as cows and horses. Hailstorms also damage roofs and windows, as well as cars and farm machinery left outdoors.

Downdrafts along the edge of a thunderstorm form what is called a gust front. These fronts are marked by strong, cold winds that blow straight down and then fan out along the earth's surface. The winds can cause a great deal of damage to homes and crops. Sometimes they kick up huge amounts of dust, blowing away topsoil and causing local dust storms.

Strong local downdrafts are called micro down-bursts or windshear. They can be especially danger-ous to aircraft. A sudden downburst can cause a plane to drop quickly, sometimes thousands of feet within seconds. The danger is even greater if an air-plane is trying to take off or land. Airports often shut down for safety reasons if downbursts are reported in the area.

Lightning is an electrical discharge within a thunderstorm. As a thunderstorm develops, the clouds become charged with electricity. Scientists are still not sure exactly what causes this to happen. But they do know that as much as 100 million volts build up in the lower part of a thunderhead, and the temperature of a single bolt of lightning reaches 50,000 degrees F. within a few millionths of a second. That's almost five times greater than the temperature at the sun's surface.

Lightning flashes when the voltage becomes high enough for electricity to leap across the air from one place to another. Lightning can spark within the cloud, from one cloud to another, from ground to cloud, or from cloud to ground.

Thunder is the sound given off by the explosive expansion of air heated by a lightning stroke. When lightning is close, thunder sounds like a single, sharp crack. From farther away, thunder sounds like a growling or rumbling noise. Thunder usually can be heard easily from six or seven miles away, and even from twenty miles away on a quiet day.

Light is about a million times faster than sound, so you see a lightning bolt almost instantly, but the sound of thunder takes about five seconds to travel one mile. This makes it possible for you to judge the distance of a lightning stroke by timing how long it takes you to hear the thunder.

Count the number of seconds between the flash and the thunder. (You can count seconds by counting slowly in this way: and a one and a two and a three and a four and a five, and so on.) Divide the number of seconds by five. The number you get is the number of miles away the lightning struck.

Lightning can be very dangerous. It causes many fires in homes and forests. It can damage power lines and sometimes black out entire cities. Lightning can also disrupt television, radio, and other kinds of communications. Every day someone, somewhere, is struck by lightning and killed or injured.

Here are some things you can do to protect yourself against lightning. If a thunderstorm threatens, go inside a house, a large building, or get into a car. Don't use a telephone except in an emergency.

If you have to stay outdoors, don't go under a large tree that stands alone. Don't stand on a hilltop or fish from a boat. Get out of and stay away from a lake, an ocean, or any other water. If you are caught on a level field, drop to your knees, bend forward, and put your hands on your knees. Don't lie down; the wet ground can carry lightning. Don't touch or go near anything metal such as a metal fence, metal pipes, railroad tracks, or a television antenna.

Sometimes a thunderstorm gives birth to a tornado. The wind blows hard and trees bend. Heavy rains or hailstones fall. Lightning and thunder rip the dark sky, and a howling roar like hundreds of jet planes fills the air.

Spinning winds inside the thunderstorm begin forming a funnel-shaped cloud that reaches downward to the ground. When it contacts the earth, an explosion of flying dirt turns the tornado dark.

This remarkable series of photos shows the life of a tornado in hours, minutes, and seconds.

As the spinning winds pick up speed, the tornado grows larger and larger. The funnel skips across the ground, sometimes setting down, sometimes bouncing upward, and then touching down again, leaving semi-circular marks on the ground like the hoofprints of giant horses. The funnel moves forward at speeds averaging thirty miles per hour, but some tornadoes

15 37 59

15 39 50

travel at more than sixty miles per hour.

Like the hose of an enormous vacuum cleaner, the tornado picks up loose materials and whirls them aloft. In less than fifteen minutes, the funnel cloud becomes clogged with dirt and air and can no longer suck up any more. The cloud becomes lighter in color as less dirt is swept aloft. As the tornado begins to lag behind the parent thunderhead, it narrows and finally vanishes altogether.

The twisting winds of a tornado whirl around the funnel at speeds of 200 miles an hour or more. Houses may be knocked down and blown apart by the wind. Then the tornado picks up the pieces, along with chairs, tables, and beds, and carries them away.

If you know a tornado is coming, go indoors, but stay away from windows. In a house, the safest place is in the cellar. Get under a table or under the stairs. If there is no cellar, go to a closet or a small room in the middle of the house. Cover yourself with a blanket or heavy towels to protect against flying glass.

Tornadoes sometimes do strange things. Once a car with two people inside was lifted to a height of 100 feet, then deposited right side up without injuring the passengers. Another tornado lifted a train locomotive from one track, spun it around in midair, and then set it down on another track facing in the opposite direction.

Hurricanes are the deadliest storms on the earth. Each year they kill more people than all other storms combined. Hurricanes are big storms that stretch

over hundreds of miles. Hurricane winds blow at least 74 miles per hour and sometimes more than 200 miles per hour. Scientists say that the energy in a hurricane is equal to dozens of atomic bombs going off every second.

Hurricanes form in the late summer over tropical seas. Water evaporates rapidly from the warm oceans, and enormous amounts of heat energy are pumped into the air. This is the breeding ground for thunder-storms that are the seedlings of hurricanes.

Once hurricanes form, they begin to travel. When they reach land, the winds pile up the water, some-times twenty feet higher than normal. Atop this dome of water are huge waves. The water crashes against the shore in what scientists call a storm surge. Beaches are washed away, and boats are sunk or car-ried inland. The howling winds bend trees and pull them right out of the ground.

Like a giant tornado, hurricane winds spin around a low-pressure center called the eye. If you are within the eye of a hurricane, the winds stop blowing, the sun shines, and the sky is blue. But the hurricane is not over. Soon the wind will be blowing from the opposite direction, just as furiously as before.

Nowadays, hurricanes — or typhoons as they are called in some places — are constantly tracked by weather satellites and radar. Above the equator, they usually travel to the north and die out over the colder waters of northern seas. Forecasters try to learn everything they can about a hurricane. They use the information to predict how the storm will move and to send warnings to communities in its path. This is a satellite photograph showing Hurricane Alicia in 1983. The white lines showing the outline of the Gulf Coast and state boundaries were added to the photograph.

There are many ancient myths about storms. The early Norsemen believed that Thor was the god of thunderstorms. They thought that lightning struck when Thor threw his mighty hammer and thunder rumbled when his chariot struck storm clouds.

Nowadays, radar, satellites, and computers keep track of storms and help scientists to forecast their behavior. But the more scientists learn about storms, the more complicated they find them to be. Storms still arouse our sense of awe and wonder.